EXPANDED VOLUME ONE

EVIL MONKEY MEMES!
EXPANDED VOLUME ONE
BY N BLAKE SEALS
ARTWORK BY BUTCH MAPA & MAURICIO LEONE

EDITED BY VINCENT FERRANTE
DESIGN AND EDITORIAL PRODUCTION BY BLAKE

MONARCHCOMICS.COM

EVIL MONKEY MAN!
IT WAS A SONG. THEN IT WAS A COMIC BOOK. NOW...IT'S A MEME.
ISN'T EVERYTHING?
THE HALLMARK OF TWENTY FIRST CENTURY INSTAGRAM PHILOSOPHY.
THE MEME.

INITIALLY A BY-PRODUCT OF PROMOTING THE COMIC, THESE MEMES,
CREATED FOR FACEBOOK, EVENTUALLY TOOK ON A LIFE OF THEIR OWN.
NOW, WITH TENS OF THOUSANDS OF LIKES AND SHARES, THEY DESERVE
A BOOK OF THEIR OWN - EVEN IF IT IS A REALLY LITTLE BOOK. ONE YOU
CAN LEAVE IN THE BATHROOM FOR COMMODIOUS ENJOYMENT ;)

SO THEN, IN THE TRADITION OF THE ONE-LINER, THE IRREVERANT
SARCASM OF THE GOTCHA, AND THE ELEVATED ART OF THE COFFEE
TABLE JOKE BOOK....PLEASE ENJOY THIS, THE VERY FIRST (*EXPANDED*)
COLLECTION OF ***EVIL MONKEY MEMES..!***

ART · BUTCH MAPA · EMM EPISODE TWO

BEFORE YOU CRITICIZE SOMEONE, YOU SHOULD WALK A MILE IN THEIR SHOES...

THAT WAY WHEN YOU CRITICIZE THEM, YOU'RE A MILE AWAY, AND YOU HAVE THEIR SHOES

ART · BUTCH MAPA · EMM EPISODE TWO

THERE ARE TWO THEORIES TO ARGUING WITH WOMEN
CLOSED
NEITHER WORK

ART · BUTCH MAPA · EMM EPISODE THREE

ALWAYS REMEMBER THAT YOU ARE UNIQUE
JUST LIKE EVERYONE ELSE

ART · BUTCH MAPA · EMM EPISODE ONE

IF AT FIRST
YOU DON'T SUCCEED
SKYDIVING IS NOT FOR YOU

ART · BUTCH MAPA · EMM EPISODE TWO

A CLEAR CONSCIENCE...
IS USUALLY A SIGN OF BAD MEMORY

ART · BUTCH MAPA · EMM EPISODE ONE & TWO

DEPRESSION IS JUST ANGER WITHOUT ENTHUSIASM

ART · BUTCH MAPA · EMM EPISODE ONE

HALF THE PEOPLE YOU KNOW...
ARE BELOW AVERAGE

ART · BUTCH MAPA · EMM EPISODE TWO

SURELY NOT EVERYBODY
WAS KUNG-FU FIGHTING?

ART · BUTCH MAPA · EMM EPISODE ONE

THAT'S A HORRIBLE IDEA
...WHAT TIME?

ART · BUTCH MAPA · EMM EPISODE TWO

NOTHING HAPPENS
WHEN YOU'RE WAITING FOR ANYTHING

ART • BUTCH MAPA • EMM EPISODE ONE

I JUST GOT LOST IN THOUGHT
IT WAS NOT FAMILIAR TERRITORY

ART · BUTCH MAPA · EMM EPISODE ONE

I FEEL LIKE I'M DIAGONALLY PARKED
IN A PARALLEL UNIVERSE

ART · BUTCH MAPA · EMM EPISODE ONE

A DAY WITHOUT SUNSHINE IS LIKE...
....NIGHT

ART · BUTCH MAPA · EMM EPISODES TWO & THREE

HONK!!
LAO SHI
IF YOU LOVE PEACE & QUIET

ART · BUTCH MAPA · EMM EPISODE THREE

A YAWN...
IS A SILENT SCREAM FOR COFFEE

ART · BUTCH MAPA · EMM EPISODE THREE

SOMETIMES...
...YOU JUST HAVE TO LET THEM HIT THEIR HEADS...

MOBIL
ART · BUTCH MAPA · EMM EPISODE TWO

GIVE A PERSON A FISH AND YOU FEED THEM FOR A DAY...
...TEACH A PERSON TO USE THE INTERNET AND THEY WON'T BOTHER YOU FOR WEEKS...MONTHS...MAYBE YEARS...

ART · BUTCH MAPA · EMM EPISODE THREE

DEATH
IS THE NUMBER ONE
KILLER IN THE WORLD

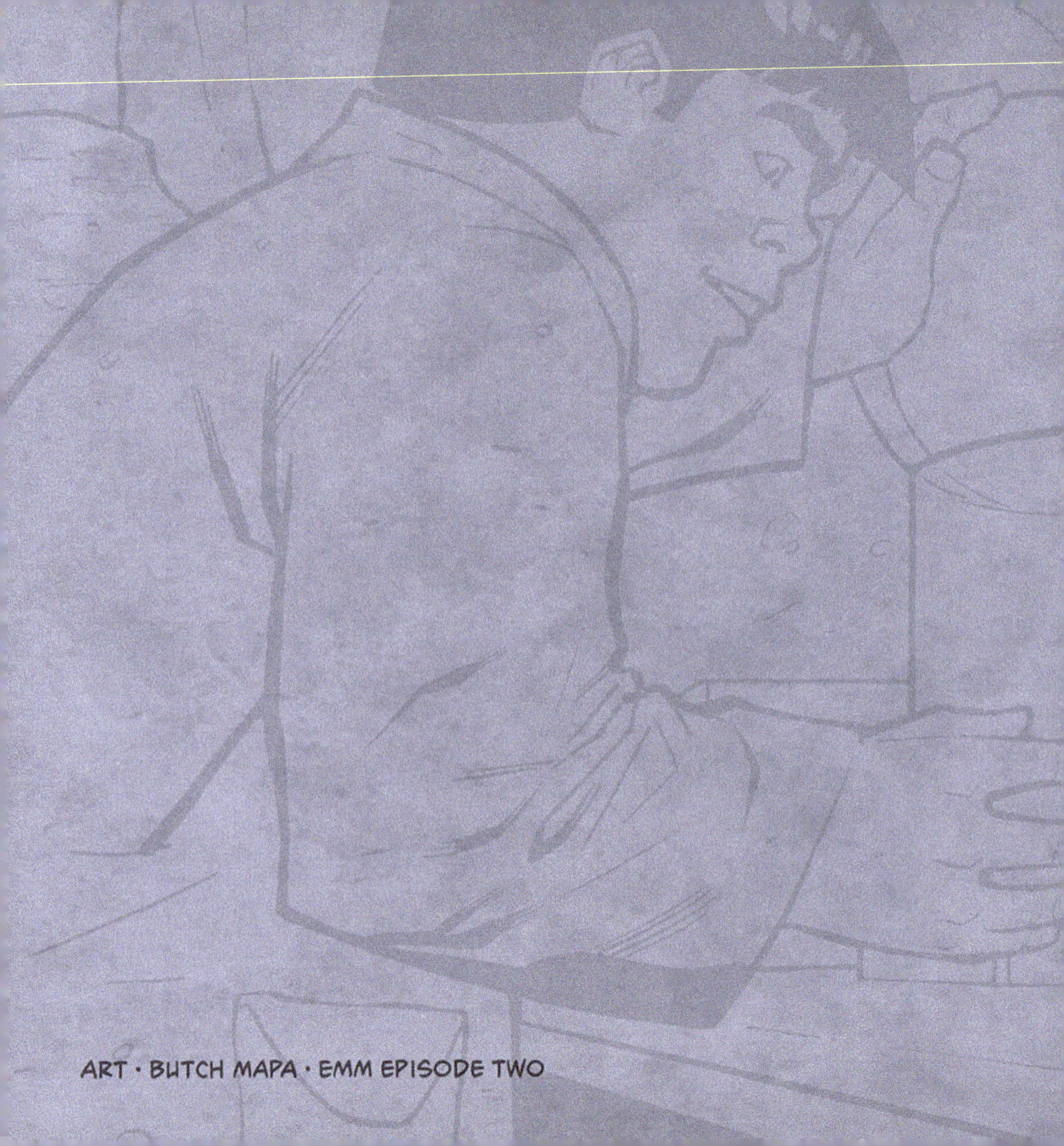

ART · BUTCH MAPA · EMM EPISODE TWO

HEALTH NUTS ARE GOING TO FEEL STUPID SOMEDAY...
...LYING IN THE HOSPITAL, DYING OF NOTHING

ART · BUTCH MAPA · EMM EPISODE THREE

IN THE 60'S, PEOPLE TOOK ACID TO MAKE THE WORLD WEIRD
NOW THE WORLD IS WEIRD AND PEOPLE TAKE PROZAC TO MAKE IT NORMAL.

ART · MAURICIO LEONE · EMM EPISODE FIVE

TURNING VEGAN...
...WOULD BE A BIG MISSED STEAK

ART · BUTCH MAPA · EMM EPISODE TWO

WHAT I IF TOLD YOU...
...YOU READ THE TOP LINE WRONG

ART · BUTCH MAPA · EMM EPISODE ONE

I HATE THE SOUND PEOPLE MAKE WHEN WORDS COME OUT OF THEIR MOUTH.

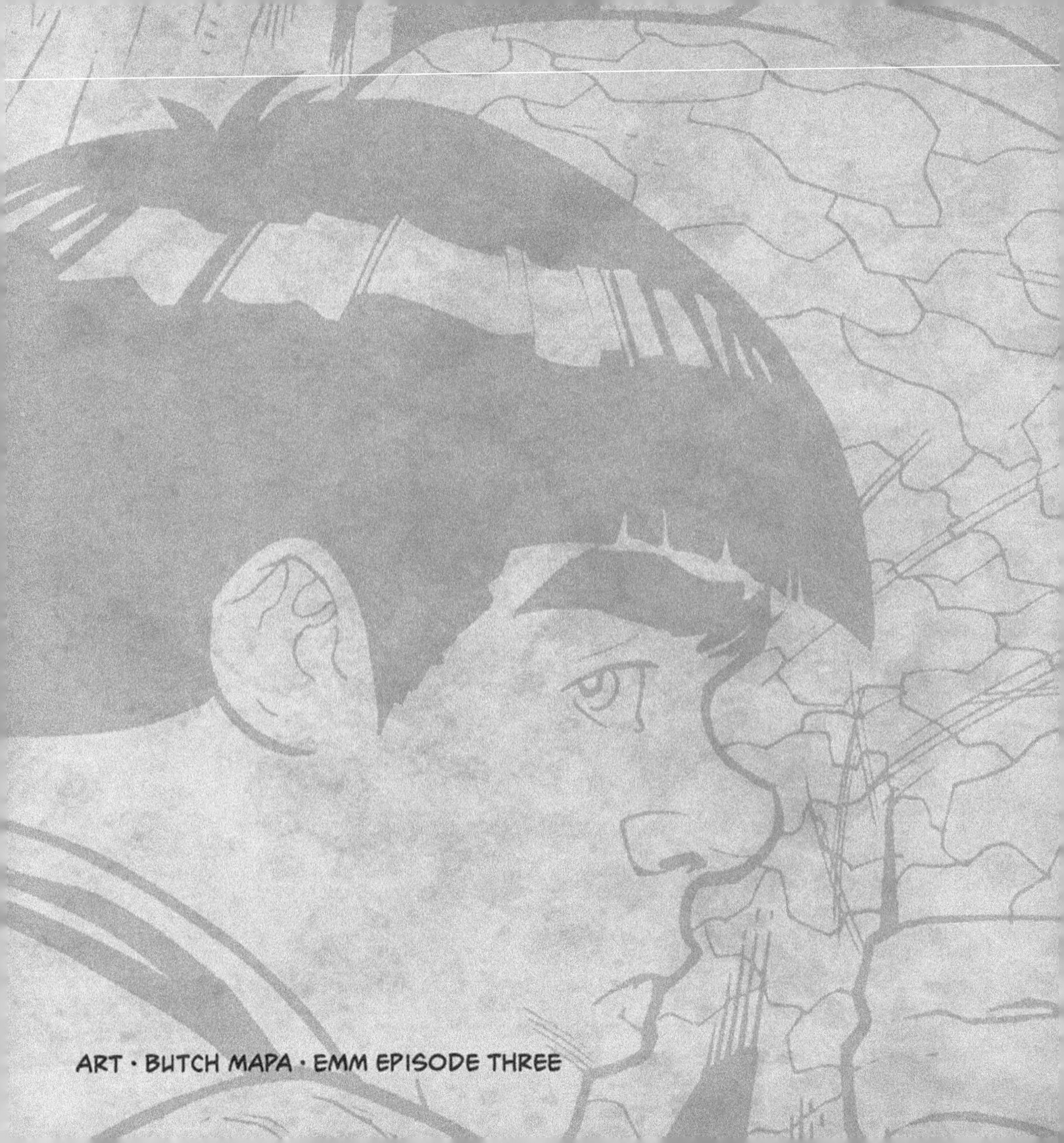

ART · BUTCH MAPA · EMM EPISODE THREE

EVERY FEW DAYS YOU SHOULD TRY YOUR ACTUAL CLOTHES ON...
...PAJAMAS WILL HAVE YOU BELIEVING THAT ALL IS WELL IN THE KINGDOM.

ART · BUTCH MAPA · EMM EPISODE FOUR

You never know what you have until it's gone...
...take toilet paper, for example.
MONARCHCOMICS.COM
©2021 N Blake Seals

ART · BUTCH MAPA · EMM EPISODE FOUR

So it turns out...
...being an adult is mostly just googling how to do stuff.
Google
MONARCHCOMICS.COM
©2021 N. Blake Seals

ART · MAURICIO LEONE · EMM EPISODE FIVE

IT'S OK IF YOU FALL APART...
...TACOS FALL APART AND WE STILL LOVE THEM.

ART · BUTCH MAPA · EMM EPISODE TWO

WHO KNEW THAT THE HARDEST PART OF BEING AN ADULT WAS GOING TO BE
FIGURING OUT WHAT TO HAVE FOR DINNER EVERY SINGLE NIGHT FOR THE REST OF YOUR LIFE UNTIL YOU DIE?!

ART · BUTCH MAPA · EMM EPISODE TWO

GOOD HEALTH...
...IS MERELY THE SLOWEST POSSIBLE RATE AT WHICH ONE CAN DIE.

ART · BUTCH MAPA · EMM EPISODE THREE

TAKE A LESSON FROM WEATHER...
...IT PAYS NO ATTENTION TO CRITICISM.

GEOLOGY ROCKS...
...BUT GEOGRAPHY IS WHERE IT'S AT.

ART · BUTCH MAPA · EMM EPISODE THREE

DUE TO UNFORTUNATE CIRCUMSTANCES...
...I'M AWAKE.

ART · BUTCH MAPA · EMM EPISODE FOUR

I'M ONE PART CONFUSED...
...AND ONE PART 'I DON'T CARE'
AND I DON'T

ART · MAURICIO LEONE · EMM EPISODE FIVE

SO...
...WHAT'S EVERYONE OVERREACTING TO TODAY?

ART · BUTCH MAPA · EMM EPISODE FOUR

THINK...
...IT'S NOT ILLEGAL YET.

ART · BUTCH MAPA · EMM EPISODE ONE

I CAN STILL REMEMBER A TIME WHEN
I WAS SMARTER THAN MY PHONE.

ART · BUTCH MAPA · EMM EPISODE TWO

HOW DARE YOU TELL ME THE TRUTH
INSTEAD OF WHAT I WANT TO HEAR?!

ART · BUTCH MAPA · EMM EPISODE THREE

EVERYONE IS DOING THE BEST THEY CAN.
WHICH IS TERRIFYING!

ART · BUTCH MAPA · EMM EPISODE FOUR

I CHOSE THE ROAD LESS TRAVELED

NOW...WHERE THE HECK AM I..?

ART · BUTCH MAPA · EMM EPISODE ONE

WELL, WELL, WELL...
...IF IT ISN'T THE CONSEQUENCES OF MY OWN ACTIONS!

ART · BUTCH MAPA · EMM EPISODE ONE

MAKE SURE YOU'RE HAPPY
IN REAL LIFE...
...NOT JUST ON INSTAGRAM.

ART · BUTCH MAPA · EMM EPISODE FOUR

PLEASE DON'T ASK ME ANYTHING IF YOU
HAVE ACCESS TO THE INTERNET.

ART · BUTCH MAPA · EMM EPISODE FOUR

THE OLDER I GET...
...THE EARLIER IT GETS LATE.

ART · MAURICIO LEONE · EMM EPISODE SIX

THEY SAY MONEY TALKS...
OPEN
...MINE ONLY SAYS "GOODBYE."

ART · BUTCH MAPA · EMM EPISODE THREE

I DON'T SUFFER FROM INSANITY...
...I ENJOY EVERY MINUTE OF IT.

WHEN TEMPTED TO FIGHT FIRE WITH FIRE, ALWAYS REMEMBER...
...THE FIRE DEPARTMENT USUALLY USES WATER.
POLICE

ART · BUTCH MAPA · EMM EPISODE TWO

TODAY A MAN KNOCKED ON MY DOOR AND ASKED FOR A SMALL DONATION TOWARDS THE LOCAL SWIMMING POOL.
I GAVE HIM A GLASS OF WATER.

ART · BUTCH MAPA · EMM EPISODE FOUR

I FIND IT IRONIC THAT THE COLORS RED, WHITE AND BLUE STAND FOR FREEDOM...
...UNTIL THEY ARE FLASHING BEHIND YOU.

ART · BUTCH MAPA · EMM EPISODE THREE

MOST PEOPLE ARE SHOCKED WHEN THEY FIND OUT HOW BAD I AM AS AN ELECTRICIAN...

ART · BUTCH MAPA · EMM EPISODE FOUR

I ACCIDENTALLY HANDED MY WIFE A GLUESTICK INSTEAD OF CHAPSTICK...
...SHE STILL ISN'T TALKING TO ME

FEATURING ARTWORK BY BUTCH MAPA & MAURICIO LEONE
FROM THE SAGA OF EVIL MONKEY MAN!
EPISODES 1 - 6
AVAILABLE AT MONARCHCOMICS.COM

THE AWARD WINNING GRAPHIC NOVEL

THE SAGA OF EVIL MONKEY MAN! SEASON ONE
BY N BLAKE SEALS & BUTCH MAPA

AVAILABLE NOW
WWW.MONARCHCOMICS.COM
AND AT FINE BOOK & COMIC BOOK STORES WORLDWIDE
INCLUDING AMAZON.COM & BARNESANDNOBEL.COM

THE PEACEFUL SERENITY OF NEW YORK SUBURB COLD SPRING HARBOR IS JOLTED WITH AN INEXPLICABLE EXPLOSION. AS FIREFIGHTERS RACE INTO BATTLE THERE ARE NOW REPORTS OF SOME SORT OF TALKING APE-MAN RUNNING AROUND TOWN.

IT'S A MIND-ALTERING, TIME-TRAVELING, REALITY-BENDING, CRISS-CROSS QUEST ACROSS AMERICA IN A SEARCH FOR A WAY TO BECOME HUMAN ONCE AGAIN.

JOIN MIKE, THE MONKEY MAN, LINA, THE KUNG-FU CHICK, MANNY, THE MUTE MIDGET, MENKE MOON, THE MAD SCIENTIST, AND DOC, THE CRUSTY NAVY CORPSMAN, AS THEY FIND THEIR WAY TO HERE THERE AND EVERYWHERE, ALL WHILE BEING PURSUED BY SOME SHADY FEDERAL AGENTS.

IT'S ALL FUN AND GAMES - UNTIL SOMEONE GETS TURNED INTO A MONKEY!

COLLECTS ISSUES 1-4 OF THE POPULAR INDIE COMIC BOOK *THE SAGA OF EVIL MONKEY MAN!* WRITTEN BY N BLAKE SEALS, ART BY BUTCH MAPA WITH COLOR BY BLAKE. COVER BY BUTCH MAPA WITH COLOR BY K MICHAEL RUSSELL.

AN IBPA BENJAMIN FRANKLIN AND PURPLE DRAGONFLY AWARD WINNER AS WELL AS A READERS' FAVORITE FIVE STAR SELECTION.

"AN ENTERTAINING, COLORFUL ADVENTURE WITH A STRIKING HERO. SEALS' BREEZY NOVEL...IS MADCAP FUN. MAPA'S ARTWORK IS PRISTINE."
   -KIRKUS REVIEWS

"IT'S FUN, FUNNY, OR BOTH. EXCELLENT ENTERTAINMENT."
   -JIM SHOOTER - LEGENDARY EDITOR-IN CHIEF OF MARVEL & VALIANT COMICS

"THE SAGA OF EVIL MONKEY MAN: SEASON ONE IS MARVELOUS, SPECTACULAR AND SO MUCH FUN TO READ. IT'S BEAUTIFULLY PUT TOGETHER: THE ART, COLORING, STORYLINE, AND THE RESULT IS A PROFESSIONALLY DESIGNED AND CREATED STORY THAT'S WACKY, ENTERTAINING, AND FILLED WITH FAST-PACED ACTION. SEALS' CHARACTERS ARE WELL-CRAFTED, AND HIS PLOT IS INGENIOUS AND CLEVER."
   -JACK MAGNUS FOR READERS' FAVORITE

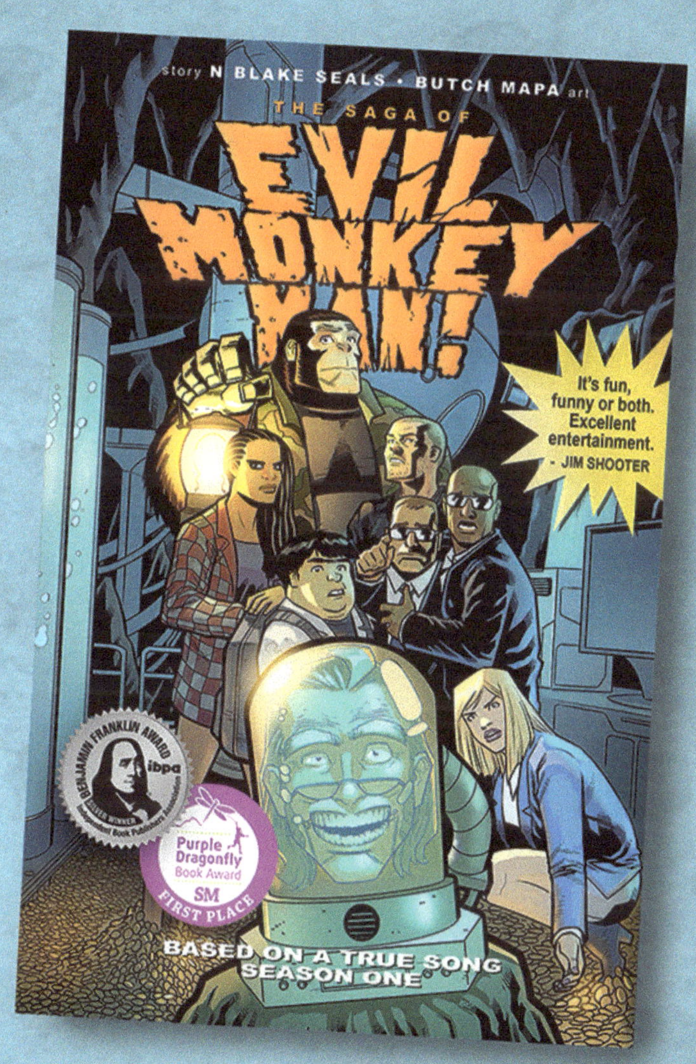

story N BLAKE SEALS • BUTCH MAPA art
THE SAGA OF
EVIL MONKEY MAN!
It's fun, funny or both. Excellent entertainment.
- JIM SHOOTER
BENJAMIN FRANKLIN AWARD
ibpa
SILVER WINNER
Independent Book Publishers Association
PURPLE DRAGONFLY Book Award
SM
FIRST PLACE
BASED ON A TRUE SONG
SEASON ONE

VOLUME TWO
ALSO AVAILABLE

MONARCHCOMICS.COM
amazon BARNES &NOBLE

EVIL MONKEY MEMES

VOL. 2

N BLAKE SEALS